Boise and La Belle Adventures

Who Needs SWIM Lessons?

S. P. Williams

Illustrated by Lizette Duvenage

Who Needs Swim Lessons?
Copyright ©2021 S. P. Williams

All rights reserved. This book or parts thereof may not be reproduced in any form, stored in any retrieval system, or transmitted in any form by any means—electronic, mechanical, photocopy, recording, or otherwise—without prior written permission of the publisher, except as provided by United States of America copyright law.

First Edition
2nd Book in the series "Boise and La Belle Adventures"

Printed in the United States of America

ISBN: 978-1-7368972-3-2 (Paperback)
ISBN: 978-1-7368972-4-9 (Hardcover)
ISBN: 978-1-7368972-5-6 (eBook Print Replica)

Library of Congress Control Number: 2021923007

Illustrated by Lizette Duvenage
Layout and Design by Becky's Graphic Design®, LLC

To Margaret, who brings kindness, patience,
and good cheer to my life.

"Who needs swim lessons?
Boise, my brother, does
but I don't."

"I can't swim, but I can splash."

"Watch me, Dad.
Splash, splash, splash!"

"La Belle, do you want to play tag?" says Boise.

"No, noo, nooo, noooo, Boise."

"I can't swim, but I can walk in the water."

"I can run in the water!"

"I can't swim, but I can float.
Well, almost."

"I can put my head under the water.
Then I can come up to breathe.
Hey, this is fun."

"O.K. Mom, watch me!
I can walk in the water and hold my breath."

"Now I can hold on to the side of the pool and kick. I can kick two ways, with straight legs or with frog legs."

"I can swim!
Sort of."

"Who needs swim lessons? Not me.

But tomorrow I'll take a lesson because swimming is fun."

About the Author

S. P. Williams is a retired librarian assistant who is currently taking line-dancing lessons, skiing on nice days, and hoping to soon resume volunteering at an animal shelter.

"Who Needs Swim Lessons?" is the second book in the series, "Boise and La Belle Adventures." The first book "Cleaning House" was released in the spring of 2021. Both books are available at your favorite online book retailers.

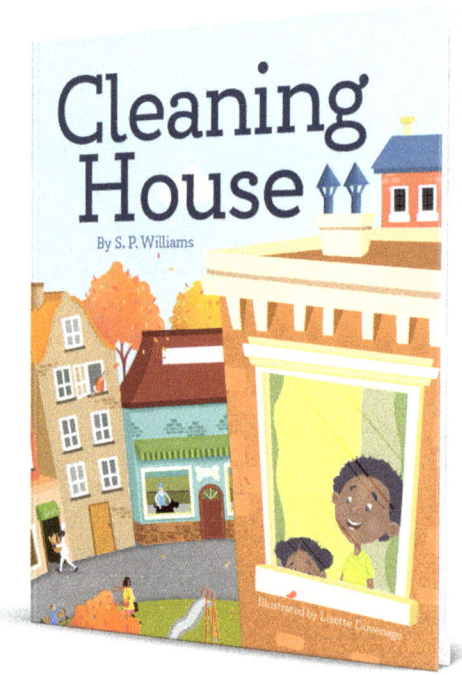

www.ingramcontent.com/pod-product-compliance
Lightning Source LLC
Chambersburg PA
CBHW051300110526
44589CB00025B/2894